"For my son Aquila. May you learn to cherish the Biblical feasts and how they point us to Jesus, our resurrected, soon returning King."
Love, Mom

The Spring Feasts

AND HOW JESUS FULFILLED THEM

Jessica AcMoody

Illustrated by Ira Baykovska

Seven feasts in all, God gave His command,
to rest, remember and yearn for His holy land.
As we gaze back in time we'll see God's mighty plan,
and get vision for Jesus, the coming Son of Man.

Each feast of our Lord, is holy and true,
God has a purpose, in each, to include you.
Let's go on a journey, we'll look to the east,
see how God's people celebrated His spring feasts.

Passover

In the nation of Egypt, a long time ago,
there was a ruler who would not let God's people go.
Trapped in slavery, the people weren't free,
But God told Pharaoh, "You must listen to me."

God sent plagues to change
Pharaoh's mind, but each time
his heart was hard and unkind.
In the final plague God had
a secret plan, to shelter His people,
and break the pride of this man.

The blood of a lamb on each Hebrew doorpost, saved God's people from the death that struck most. Finally, oh finally, God's people were free, and He led them to safety across the Red Sea.

This special, remarkable story points to Jesus,
God's only Son who came to save each of us.
To free us from sin, that traps us like slaves,
and lead us to walk in new life He displayed.
He's the Passover lamb, blood shed for you and me,
He died and rose again so we could fully be free.

Feast of Unleavened Bread

Before God's people left Egypt, He gave
a command, "Take bread without leaven,
then leave for the Promised Land."
"Remove all the leaven!" God's people
were told, "Sweep the house clean,
remove it all from the fold."

So, the people left with haste, no time for the bread to rise,
a swift flight from Egypt, the back-breaking work and cries.
The leaven was like sin, puffing up their hearts,
God wanted to give His people a brand-new start.

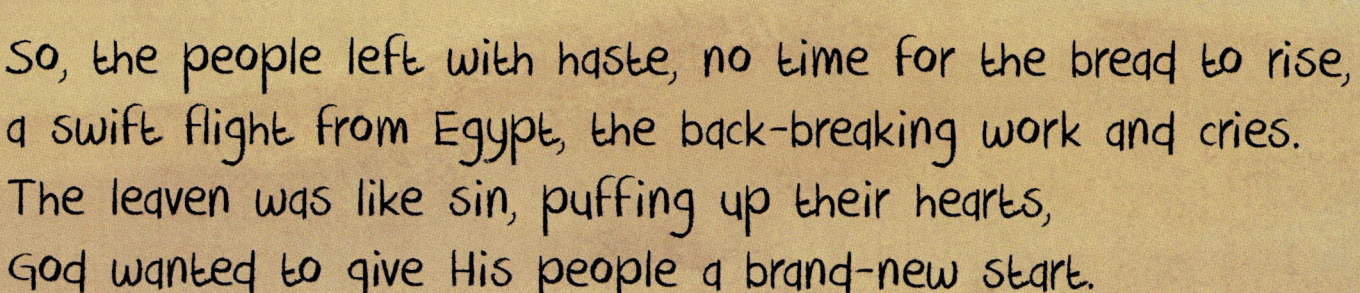

Abraham

Isaac — Jacob — Judah — Perez — Hetron — Ra

Uzziaz — Joram — Johoshaphat — Asa — Abija

Jotham — Ahaz — Hezekiah —

For God's people this special moment in time
points towards Jesus who descended from Jesse's line.
Jesus, bread of life, His body broken for all, freedom
for us, no more sin - our downfall.

Feast of First Fruits

When God brought His people into the Promised
Land, He gave a decree, another command.
"Bring the first fruits of the land straight to the priest,
an offering of thanksgiving, he will wave the sheaf."

Thanksgiving to the Lord for His mighty deeds,
meant offering the first fruits of all crops and trees.
The people were so glad to freely worship the Lord,
with fertile land, crops aplenty, their hearts soared.

Jesus is our first fruit, He rose from the dead, the promise of eternal life, and resurrection He led. This Feast of First Fruits points to a great day, the resurrection of all who trust and obey.

About the Author

Jessica AcMoody is a wife and stay at home mother of two.
Through a small web based ministry she enjoys creating and sharing resources for families to grow together in the Lord.

For a decade, before becoming a mother, she was an urban Christian school educator. Serving first as an elementary school teacher at Tree of Life School in Kalamazoo, MI and then as elementary school principal and founder of River of Life School in Benton Harbor, MI.

You can follow her ministry page «Elemental Faith» on both Facebook and Instagram for more resources and Biblebased content.

About the Illustrator

Ira Baykovska is a children's book illustrator and a mom of two beautiful girls.

Ira has been drawing for as long as she can remember and sometimes cannot believe that this hobby has become her life-long career.

She has been working as a freelance illustrator since 2014 and has illustrated more than 20 books for kids. Ira has a degree in Graphic Design and currently lives and works in Lviv, Ukraine.

Visit Ira's website **www.baykovska.com**

Made in the USA
Coppell, TX
25 March 2025

47556303R00019